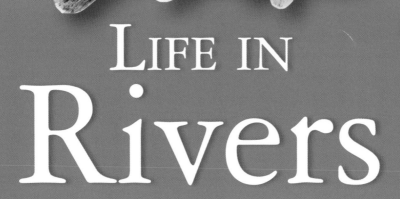

LIFE IN
Rivers

BY MIRELLA S. MILLER

The Child's World®

Published by The Child's World®
1980 Lookout Drive • Mankato, MN 56003-1705
800-599-READ • www.childsworld.com

Acknowledgments
The Child's World®: Mary Berendes, Publishing Director
Red Line Editorial: Editorial direction
The Design Lab: Design
Amnet: Production

Design Elements: Evlakhov Valeriy/Shutterstock Images; Pan Xunbin/Shutterstock Images

Photographs ©: Nicola Margaret/iStockphoto, cover (center), 1 (center); Evlakhov Valeriy/Shutterstock Images, cover, 1 (top); Pan Xunbin/Shutterstock Images, cover, 1; Cedric Weber/Shutterstock Images, 4–5; Janne Hamalainen/Shutterstock Images, 6; Shutterstock Images, 8, 13, 17, 19, 21, 21(top left), 21 (center), 21 (middle left); Background Land/Shutterstock Images, 11; Hung Chung Chih/Shutterstock Images, 14; Filip Fuxa/Shutterstock Images, 21 (middle right); IRC/Shutterstock Images, 21 (bottom right)

ISBN 9781626872998
LCCN 2014930652

Printed in the United States of America
Mankato, MN
July, 2014
PA02218

ABOUT THE AUTHOR

Mirella S. Miller is a writer and editor who lives in Minnesota. She likes to take her dog for walks by the Mississippi River.

CONTENTS

Welcome to a River

It is a busy morning at the riverbank. Willow tree branches move with the wind. Bank swallows fly back and forth across the river. A bobcat watches the

water for a trout. A salamander digs in the sand for a worm. He is hungry. Playful otters float down the river, too.

This river is a water biome. A biome is a place in nature that supports certain types of life. Plants and animals of a biome are specially suited to live there. Let's learn more about the river biome!

River otters live both on land and in the water.

What Is a River?

A river is a body of water that moves over land. The water moves in one direction. The river's **current** can be fast or slow.

Rivers are found around the world. They are on every continent and on all kinds of land. You may

The Amazon River flows through many countries in South America.

see a river in a **canyon**. Or you may see one in a jungle. Many plants and animals live in or near rivers.

All rivers are not the same size or length. Some rivers are wide. Other rivers are skinny. Sometimes a river is wide in one spot. Then it changes shape. Shorter rivers may flow together to become a longer river. Some rivers are very long. They flow across a whole continent. Most rivers flow all year long. Other rivers only flow during rainy seasons.

Although rivers are different, they all start at a high point. The high point may be a mountain or a hill. Some river water comes from lakes. It can also come from rainwater or melting snow. The water flows down from the high point. It gathers more water as it moves. The more water it gathers, the wider the river becomes.

The Amazon River is the longest river in the world. It moves across South America. The river is at least 4,000 miles (6,437 km) long.

Parts of a River

Rivers have many parts. A river's water **source** is at its highest point. This is also called its **headwaters**.

A river is small at its headwaters. It is more like a stream. Rainwater adds to the river. Other small

The Colorado River turns at Horseshoe Bend.

rivers feed into the river. These small rivers are its **tributaries**. Large rivers have many tributaries. The Amazon River in South America has more than 1,000 tributaries.

A river ends at its mouth. This is where a river flows into a larger body of water. Some rivers empty into lakes. Other rivers empty into oceans.

Rivers also have an upper, middle, and lower course. The upper course has steep valleys and waterfalls. The river moves fast in this area. The water carves rock as it moves. This changes the land. The Colorado River carved the Grand Canyon in North America. It started carving the rock more than 17 million years ago.

The middle course is the widest part of the river. The water usually flows slowly here. Some rivers have a strong current in the middle course, though. The Congo River in Africa has a powerful middle course. The lower course is at the mouth of a river. The land near the lower course is flat.

At the Source

A river's source affects the entire body of water.
Animals and plants need a healthy home.
If **pollutants** are in the headwaters, they will ruin
the river.

The water temperature at the source is colder than
at the mouth. Freshwater fish, such as trout, live at the
source. The water is full of **oxygen**. Fish need oxygen
to breathe below water. They eat young insects that
live in the sand and rocks. Water striders feed on tiny
fish and other insects. These insects leave the water
when they are adults.

Green river grasses grow in the river. They have
strong roots planted in the
ground. Grasses and other
plants use **photosynthesis** to
grow. They turn sunlight into
food energy. Snails crawl along

Caddis flies glue
sand and small
rocks to their bodies.
This hides them
from **predators**.

plant stems. Female frogs stick their eggs to plants. This keeps the eggs in place. The water cannot move them. When the frog tadpoles hatch, they hide among the plants. They do not want to be eaten by fish.

Wild rainbow trout are native to rivers and lakes in North America.

The Riverbank

The edges of rivers are its riverbanks. This includes the ground above a river and leading down to a river.

Trees are common near rivers. Cottonwoods grow nearby. Willows, elms, and oaks tower along the banks. Brazil nut trees grab the most sunlight along the Amazon River. Papyrus trees grow along the Nile River's banks.

Many plants grow under the tree cover. Ferns and flowers become food for animals. Other animals hide among the plants. They do not want to become food for bigger animals.

The riverbanks can also be animals' homes. Bank swallows dig their nests in a river's steep sides. The birds peek out of their nests and watch for food. Mosquitoes and other insects are their favorites. Salamanders and newts also hunt for insects.

Large mammals visit a riverbank in search of food and water. Raccoons and bobcats watch the water. They look for plump fish. Hippopotamuses cool off in African rivers.

Bank swallows return to their nests along a riverbank.

River Otters

North American river otters make homes near the river, too. River otters easily go from land to water. Otter dens are empty beaver homes or hollow logs.

Otters hunt for fish, eggs, frogs, and other animals by the river.

The den's openings are covered with tree roots and thick plants. Some otter dens have underwater entrances.

North American river otters can dive up to 45 feet (14 m)!

River otters have long bodies, strong legs, and long tails. They also have webbed feet. Their bodies help them swim well. River otters spend most of their lives in the water. They hunt for fish and crayfish. Slow-moving fish, like bullheads, are easy for otters to catch. They carry the fish to shore to eat. They do not have to worry about predators. River otters are strong and have sharp teeth. They can also hide in their underground dens.

River otters are playful animals. They like to toss rocks to each other. River otters also slide down snowy banks.

The Middle of a River

The middle is the deepest part of a river. Some animals live on the riverbank but spend time in the river's water. Turtles hunt for food in the river. But they live on the riverbank. Crayfish are one animal that only lives in the river.

The current is fast and strong in the river's middle. The sculpin fish uses its fins to fight the current. Its fins grab on to rocks to stay in place. Many large animals search the rocks for fish. The sculpin's skin blends in with the river bottom. Other animals cannot see the fish.

Crayfish use their claws to crawl along the river bottom. They search for **algae**. Snapping turtles also move along the bottom. They hunt for fish, green plants, and other food.

Some larger mammals also live in rivers. Indus river dolphins live in the Indus River in Asia.

The Amazon river dolphin can only live in freshwater.

These river dolphins grow to be 8.2 feet (2.5 m) long. They hunt for catfish, carp, and other animals. River dolphins live in other major rivers as well. A pink river dolphin lives in the Amazon River.

The Mouth of a River

The water is cloudy in the mouth of a river. As the river flows from its source, it picks up sand, clay, and rocks. The sand, clay, and rocks sink to the river's bottom near the mouth.

Sunlight cannot reach the bottom since the water is cloudy. Fewer plants grow at the mouth. Plants create oxygen during photosynthesis. Without many plants, there is less oxygen. Fish and other animals learn to live with little oxygen.

Seaweed and river grasses are among the few plants that do grow at the mouth of the river. Fish hide among the roots. They also feed on the plants.

The mouth of a river is a common spot for walleye. The water is calm here. Walleye hunt for smaller fish to eat. Bass are also found at the mouth.

The cloudy water of a river's mouth flows into a lake.

The River Food Chain

Rivers are filled with life. Each plant and animal is important to a river's food chain. This is the way that plants and animals work together in a habitat.

A river's food chain starts with the sun. Sunlight reaches the river. Plants use the sunlight to create energy and oxygen. Seaweed, algae, and papyrus grow. Snails eat algae. Many other animals feed on the plants. Fish eat insects, snails, and plants. Otters, river dolphins, and bobcats feed on insects and fish in a river. A hippopotamus comes to a river for water. It may also search for food.

Each plant and animal is important to a river. They work together to create a healthy home. Without one plant or animal, a river biome would not be the same.

In one type of river food chain, algae uses energy from the sun to grow, snails eat algae, bullhead fish eat snails, and otters eat bullhead fish.

GLOSSARY

algae (AL-jee) Algae are small simple plants without roots or stems. Crayfish feed on algae.

canyon (KAN-yuhn) A canyon is a deep valley with steep sides and a river flowing through it. A river carved the Grand Canyon.

current (KUR-uhntz) A current is the movement of water over a certain direction. A river's current can be fast or slow.

headwaters (HED-waw-turs) A river's headwaters is where it begins. A river's headwaters is its source of water.

oxygen (OK-suh-juhn) Oxygen is a colorless, tasteless, and odorless gas. Fish breathe oxygen through the water.

photosynthesis (foh-toh-SIN-thi-sis) Photosynthesis is the process plants use to convert sunlight into food energy. Grasses and trees use photosynthesis to grow.

pollutants (puh-LOOT-uhnts) Pollutants are things that spoil a natural resource. Pollutants destroy the water in a river.

predators (PRED-uh-turs) Predators are animals that hunt other animals for food. Many river insects hide from predators.

source (SORSS) A source is the beginning of a stream of water. A river's source can be a lake.

tributaries (TRIB-yuh-ter-ees) Tributaries are rivers that flow into a larger river or a lake. The Amazon River has more than 1,000 tributaries.

TO LEARN MORE

BOOKS

Crewe, Sabrina. *In Rivers, Lakes, and Ponds.*
New York: Chelsea Clubhouse, 2010.

Gray, Leon. *Rivers*. New York: Rosen Publishing, 2011.

Lynette, Rachel. *Giant River Otters*. New York: Bearport Publishing, 2013.

WEB SITES

Visit our Web site for links about the river biome:
childsworld.com/links

Note to Parents, Teachers, and Librarians: We routinely verify our Web links to make
sure they are safe and active sites. So encourage your readers to check them out!

INDEX